D0460659

Oils, Lotions & Other Luxuries

Oils, Lotions & Other Luxuries

Make Beautiful Gifts to Give (or Keep)

KELLY RENO

PRIMA PUBLISHING

PRIMA PUBLISHING, its colophon, and GOOD GIFTS FROM THE HOME are trademarks of Prima Publishing, a division of Prima Communications, Inc.

DISCLAIMER: THE EXPRESS PURPOSE OF *OILS, LOTIONS & OTHER LUXURIES* IS TO PROVIDE SUGGESTIONS FOR A RECREATIONAL HOBBY. THE AUTHOR AND PUBLISHER DISCLAIM ANY WARRANTY OR GUARANTEE, EXPRESS OR IMPLIED, FOR ANY OF THE RECIPES OR FORMULAS CONTAINED HEREIN AND FURTHER DISCLAIM ANY LIABILITY FOR THE READER'S EXPERIMENTS OR PROJECTS. THE AUTHOR AND PUBLISHER DO NOT ASSUME ANY LIABILITY FOR ANY DAMAGES THAT MAY OCCUR AS A RESULT OF READING OR FOL-LOWING ANY OF THE RECIPES OR FORMULAS IN THIS BOOK. THE PURCHASE OF THIS BOOK BY THE READER WILL SERVE AS AN ACKNOWLEDGMENT OF THIS DISCLAIMER AND AN AGREEMENT TO HOLD THE AUTHOR AND PUBLISHER HARMLESS FOR ANY MISTAKES THE READER MAY MAKE AS A RESULT OF FOLLOWING THE RECIPES AND FORMULAS IN THIS BOOK.

Library of Congress Cataloging-in-Publication Data

Reno, Kelly.
   Oils, lotions & other luxuries / by Linda Ferrari.
      p.   cm. — (Good gifts from the home)

   Includes index.
   ISBN 0-7615-0334-X
   1. Cosmetics.   2. Title.   3. Series.
TP983.R38 1996   95-44916
668'.5—dc20   CIP

96 97 98 99 00 AA 10 9 8 7 6 5 4 3 2 1

Printed in the United States of America

HOW TO ORDER:
Single copies may be ordered from Prima Publishing, P.O. Box 1260BK, Rocklin, CA 95677; telephone (916) 632-4400. Quantity discounts are also available. On your letterhead, include information concerning the intended use of the books and the number of books you wish to purchase.

Dedicated with love to the Reno women
Catherine, Kathleen, Jenny, Caroline, Shannon, Sarah, and Little Shannon.

CONTENTS

GIVING GIFTS is an act of beauty in itself, representing friendship and love. What better gifts to give than homemade beauty products! In this book you'll find more than fifty recipes for creamy lotions, silky oils, and many other luxurious formulas that delight the senses and please almost everyone. There's nothing more personal than a gift that you've made yourself. Hand-crafting your own gifts shows that you care and have invested thought and time, making them all the more special. With my tried-and-true recipes, your friends and family will be delighted with your creations and will probably request a second batch.

The unique formulas in this book are made from natural ingredients. Through my research, I was able to locate and replace the chemical ingredients (found in most manufactured products) with safe and healthy substitutes. All of my original recipes have a decent shelf life without the use of preservatives and require no special care such as refrigeration. The finished formulas are as good as (if not better than) commercially prepared products on the market. You'll also find that making cosmetics yourself may save you hundreds of dollars a year! Anyone can make exquisite gifts from ordinary things, as the recipes prove. Whether for a birthday, holiday, or any occasion, you'll find the perfect present for everyone in your list here in these pages. Don't forget to save some for yourself!

I've learned through trial and error, so let me offer you some hints where to find these ingredients. Floral waters can be found at some gourmet cooking stores. Fuller's earth, mineral oil, borax, liquid glycerin, and witch hazel are available at drugstores. Liquid lanolin, aloe vera gel, tea tree oil, and fragrance oils can be purchased from health food stores that carry beauty supplies. Beeswax can be purchased from a candle-making supply store. I've also added a marketplace section so you can order sometimes hard-to-find ingredients by mail if you don't happen to live in a big city where these things are readily available. The research is done and the recipes are ready for you to use. Enjoy!

Oils, Lotions & Other Luxuries

CHAPTER ONE

Lotions, Creams & Moisturizers

LOTIONS AND creamy moisturizers are luxurious gifts. The first lotions were made by the ancient Greeks. The original formula was made from a mixture of oil, beeswax, and water. It was applied to the skin, to create a feeling of coolness, and was discovered to retain moisture. Today, lotions, creams, and moisturizers are still made from similar formulations and are used to retain moisture and prevent dry skin.

❧ *To make a custom fragranced cream or lotion, replace the suggested fragrance oil with an equal amount of your fragrance oil of choice.*
❧ *When making lotions and creams it is imperative to add the water/borax mixture into the oil/wax mixture very slowly—about a teaspoonful at a time—to avoid separation.*

This thick, moisture-rich cold cream is a pampering remedy for dry skin. This recipe is an updated version of a beeswax beauty cream developed by the ancient Greeks. They used a similar recipe to soften the skin and keep it young looking. After cleansing the face, soothe it on at night for a super moisturizing treatment or keep it refrigerated for a cool treat on hot nights.

Makes 8 ounces

> ¼ cup distilled water
> ⅛ teaspoon borax powder
> 3 tablespoons beeswax, grated
> ½ cup mineral oil
> 1 teaspoon coconut oil
> 15 drops fragrance oil (optional)

Boil the water in a saucepan and add the borax powder, stirring until dissolved. Simmer while preparing the next step. In a separate, heavy saucepan over low heat, add the mineral oil, coconut oil, and beeswax and stir until the wax has dissolved. Pour the oil/beeswax mixture into a ceramic bowl and slowly add the heated water/borax mixture while stirring with a wire whisk. Continue stirring until the mixture becomes a thick, white cream and has cooled to room temperature. Stir in the fragrance oil (if desired). Spoon into a wide-mouth jar and seal.

VANILLA BODY LOTION

This deliciously fragrant lotion captures the essence of pure vanilla. With a light, subtle scent it is ideal for all your skin's moisturizing needs.

Makes 8 ounces

¼ cup distilled water
1 teaspoon pure vanilla extract
½ teaspoon borax powder
3 tablespoons beeswax, grated
¼ cup mineral oil
¼ cup sweet almond oil
20 drops vanilla fragrance oil

Bring the water and vanilla extract to a boil in a saucepan and add the borax, stirring until dissolved. In a separate, heavy saucepan, combine the beeswax, mineral oil, and almond oil and stir until the beeswax has melted. Remove from heat. Slowly pour the heated water and borax mixture into the oil and beeswax mixture, with constant stirring. Continue to stir until the mixture becomes a thick cream and has cooled to room temperature. Stir in the vanilla fragrance oil. Pour into a bottle and close.

. . . .

This fragrant, heavy-duty cream is a favorite of gardeners because of its thick, coating texture. It can also be used as a body moisturizer to handle and protect problem dry areas such as elbows and knees. To make an unscented cream, delete the fragrance oil. You can also substitute the peach and berry fragrance oils with ten drops of your favorite fragrance oil.

Makes 8 ounces

    ½ cup distilled water
    ⅛ teaspoon borax powder
    ⅓ cup sweet almond oil
    1 tablespoon beeswax, grated
    1 teaspoon liquid lanolin
    1 teaspoon coconut oil
    10 drops fragrance oil (use 5 drops raspberry and 5 drops peach)

. . . .

Combine the water and borax in a heavy saucepan over low heat and stir until the borax has dissolved. In a separate saucepan, melt the beeswax and add the almond oil, coconut oil, and liquid lanolin, stirring the mixture until all ingredients are well blended. Remove from heat. Slowly pour the heated water/borax mixture into the oil/beeswax mixture while stirring constantly. Continue stirring until the mixture forms a thick, white cream and has cooled to room temperature. Stir in fragrance oil. Pour into a jar or bottle and seal.

This moisturizer is ideal for after a bath or any time you need a refreshing lift. Super Light Honeydew Moisturizer was developed to replenish the skin's moisture without heavy, greasy elements.

Makes 10 ounces

> ½ cup orange flower water
> ½ cup distilled water
> 1 teaspoon borax powder
> ¼ cup apricot kernel oil
> 2 teaspoons beeswax, grated
> 15 drops honeydew fragrance oil

Bring the orange flower water and distilled water to a boil in a saucepan and add the borax powder, stirring until dissolved. In a separate saucepan, heat the apricot oil and add the beeswax, stirring until the wax has melted. Remove from heat. Slowly pour the heated water and borax mixture into the oil and beeswax mixture with constant stirring. Continue stirring until a light, white cream forms and the mixture has cooled to room temperature. Add the fragrance oil and stir well. Pour the cream into a squeeze bottle or spray-pump bottle and cap tightly. Shake before use.

❖ *For a floral variation, replace the orange flower water with rose water and the honeydew fragrance oil with rose or jasmine, or any floral fragrance oil you prefer.*

LEMON MERINGUE PIE LOTION

. . . .

This naturally fragrant lotion is perfect for the face and body. Its citrus elements will help to exfoliate dry skin gently while the rich, nourishing oils leave the skin feeling silky smooth. The concept of this cream dates back to the Victorian era, when women commonly used blends of citrus fruit to lighten their skin. This particular lotion is comparable to creams on the market that help the skin shed away dead cells to reveal a new, fresher layer. This cream also helps diminish the appearance of fine lines over time.

Makes 6 ounces

      2 tablespoons beeswax, grated
      ¼ cup coconut oil
      2 tablespoons apricot kernel oil
      ¼ teaspoon lemon oil
      2 tablespoons liquid glycerin
      2 tablespoons distilled water
      1 teaspoon borax powder

Melt the beeswax and all oils in a heavy saucepan over low heat and stir until the wax dissolves. Stir in the glycerin and continue to simmer while doing the next step. In a separate, small pan, boil the water and add the borax powder, stirring until dissolved. Slowly pour the hot water and borax mixture into the oil and beeswax mixture, stirring constantly with a wire whisk. Continue to stir until the mixture forms a thick, white cream and has cooled to room temperature. Bottle.

PEPPERMINT CREAM

This fragrant cream made with pure peppermint oil is a stimulating formula, ideal for all-over moisturizing. Peppermint Cream leaves the skin feeling fresh and can help to increase circulation.

Makes 8 ounces

  ½ cup distilled water
  1 teaspoon borax powder
  ⅓ cup coconut oil
  1 tablespoon liquid lanolin
  1 tablespoon beeswax, grated
  2 teaspoons sweet almond oil
  15 drops peppermint oil
  1 drop red food coloring (optional)

In a saucepan, bring the water to a boil and add the borax, simmer and stir until dissolved. In a second, heavy saucepan over low heat, combine the coconut oil, lanolin, beeswax, and almond oil, stirring until the wax has melted. Remove from heat. Slowly pour the water and borax mixture into the oils while stirring with a wire whisk. Continue stirring until the mixture thickens and has cooled to room temperature. Stir in the peppermint oil and food coloring (if desired) until well blended. Pour into a bottle and close.

✦ *This silky cream is perfect for massage or try rubbing this formula into the feet after a long day.*

✦ *A wonderful shaving cream can be made from this recipe (see Peppermint Latherless Shaving Cream).*

OIL-FREE MOISTURIZER

This moisturizer is ideal for a light, skin-rejuvenating treat, especially for those with oily skin who don't need extra oil. The skin soaks up this moisture-rich formula made with aloe vera.

Makes 7 ounces

½ cup aloe vera gel
¼ cup distilled water
2 tablespoons orange flower water

Combine all ingredients in a bowl and stir with a wire whisk until well blended. Bottle.

SPORTS CREAM

....

This all-natural cream is ideal for applying to sore muscles after a tough workout. The recipe is based on an ancient Asian formula developed more than one hundred years ago to relieve minor muscle aches.

Makes 4 ounces

> ½ cup The Original Skin Cream
>   (see recipe on page 2)
> 10 drops camphor oil
> 5 drops peppermint oil
> 5 drops wintergreen oil

Add oils to The Original Skin Cream. Stir until well blended. Store in a wide-mouthed jar.

CHAPTER TWO

Oils

OVER THE CENTURIES, people have found a multitude of uses for oils extracted from plants. Both ancient and modern cultures use oils in medicinal practices. They are also used in lotions, creams, shampoos, for massage and moisturizing, and in the practice of aromatherapy.

Essential oils are extracted directly from a plant, flower, or herb. Many of the essential oils retain the fragrance of their source. A good example is lemon oil, which is extracted from the peel of the fruit. Essential oils differ from *perfume oils*, which are synthetic fragrances in a base of unscented oil. Perfume oils have no value to the human body except for the purpose of fragrancing.

In this chapter you will find many recipes for oil blends specially formulated for massage and moisturizing, or for handling special problems such as stretch marks and wrinkles.

WRINKLE-SMOOTHING POTION

◈ *This blend of almond, jojoba, vitamin E oil, and lanolin will help to smooth out and lessen the appearance of fine lines on the face. Rub a small amount into the skin at night and let this potion work its magic.*

Makes 1 ounce

> 1 tablespoon almond oil
> 1 tablespoon liquid lanolin
> 1 tablespoon jojoba oil
> ¼ teaspoon vitamin E oil

Combine all ingredients in a bowl and stir until well mixed. Pour into a wide-mouthed jar and seal.

◈ *A great gift for anyone celebrating a thirtieth, fortieth, or fiftieth birthday!*

. . . .

◈ *This special blend of oils helps prevent and reduce the appearance of unsightly stretch marks on the skin. Stretch Mark Miracle Oil is especially recommended for anyone dieting or losing weight, and especially for expectant mothers during and after pregnancy. The oil can also be applied to existing stretch marks to help restore elasticity.*

Makes 3½ ounces

> ¼ cup coconut oil
> 2 tablespoons cocoa butter
> 2 teaspoons sweet almond oil

In a heavy saucepan over low heat, warm the coconut oil, cocoa butter, and almond oil. Stir until the mixture is well blended and clear. Remove from heat. Store in a wide-mouth jar.

◈ *Stretch Mark Miracle Oil is the perfect (and economical) gift to give at a baby shower to the expecting mom! This oil should be stored at 76°F for best results.*

RICH MOISTURIZING OIL

This blend of oils is perfect for locking moisture into the skin after a bath or any time the skin feels dry. Fragrance oil can be added to this formula if you desire a light scent.

Makes 4½ ounces

> ¼ cup sesame oil
> ¼ cup safflower oil
> 1 tablespoon jojoba oil
> ¼ teaspoon fragrance oil of choice

Combine all oils in a bowl and stir until well mixed. Bottle and store in a cool place.

Great for massage.

FIVE-OIL MASSAGE BLEND

This long-lasting body oil is perfect for massage or after a bath. Five special oils have been chosen for this luxurious blend. Add a few drops of your favorite fragrance oil to make a customized formula.

Makes 5 ounces

    ¼ cup avocado oil
    2 tablespoons sweet almond oil
    2 tablespoons apricot kernel oil
    2 tablespoons olive oil
    5 drops fragrance oil (optional)

Combine all ingredients in a bowl and stir until well blended. Bottle and store in a cool place.

SPRAY-ON BODY OIL

This delightful formula solves the problem of applying messy oils to the body. A unique combination of rose water and body-silkening oils help the skin retain vital moisture. Spray on for long-lasting softness.

Makes 6 ounces

¼ cup vodka
¼ cup rose water
3 tablespoons sweet almond oil
1 teaspoon jojoba oil

Pour all ingredients into a spray-pump bottle and close. Shake the bottle until well mixed. Give the bottle a shake before each use.

CHAPTER THREE

For the Bath

BATHING IS a time to relax and refresh our bodies. There's something calming and almost magical about sinking into a tub full of warm water at the end of the day. By adding soothing oils and other fragrant ingredients to the water, it creates a wonderful little escape. From relaxing salts and fragrant bath beads to deliciously scented dusting powders, you'll find a recipe in this chapter for everyone. And remember: A sampling of bath formulas wrapped up in a decorative basket makes a wonderful gift.

RELAXING BATH OIL

Relaxing Bath Oil has been specially blended to relax the senses and leave the skin feeling soft and silky. Pure essences of orange, sandalwood, and jasmine were chosen for their calming effects.

Makes 4 ounces

> ½ cup sweet almond oil oil
> 10 drops sandalwood oil
> 5 drops jasmine oil
> 5 drops orange oil

Combine all oils in a bowl and stir until well blended. Bottle.

To use, pour one tablespoon into a tub full of warm water.

HERBAL TEA BATH

....

◈ *Turn your bath into a giant cup of soothing herbal tea. The herbs in this recipe delight the senses and soothe the body. Wrapped up in ribbon and lace, these decorative bath bags make delightful gifts.*

Makes 1 bag

   2 tablespoons dried chamomile
   2 tablespoons dried rose petals
   2 tablespoons dried orange blossoms
   1 coffee filter
   One 8-inch by 8-inch piece of lace fabric
   One 20-inch piece of satin ribbon

Combine the chamomile, rose petals, and orange blossoms in a bowl and stir until well mixed. Spoon the herbs into the coffee filter and secure by tying with a piece of embroidery thread or ribbon. Place the coffee filter bag in the center of the lace. Gather together the edges of the lace and secure by tying and knotting the ribbon around it. Tie the ends of the ribbon in another knot at the top (so that the ribbon forms a large loop that can be hung from the bathtub water spout.)

◈ *To use, hang the bag from the water spout and let it steep in the warm bath water. Do not reuse the bag.*

....

FLORAL SPA BATH

....

◈ *This specially designed bath treatment combines the benefits of hydrotherapy and aromatherapy. The mineral-rich sea salts and cleansing baking soda come together in a bouquet of floral scents that will turn your bath into a luxurious escape that restores moisture to the skin.*

Makes 5 ounces

> ¼ cup sea salt
> ¼ cup borax powder
> 2 tablespoons baking soda
> 5 drops lavender oil
> 5 drops jasmine oil

Combine the salt, borax, and baking soda in a bowl, stirring until well blended. Add the lavender and jasmine oils and stir until evenly distributed throughout the mixture. (Crush any remaining lumps with the back of a spoon.)

◈ *To use, pour two ounces into warm bath water.*
◈ *Wrap individual packets of Floral Spa Bath in decorative envelopes made out of wrapping paper.*

....

ROSE BATH BEADS

⬧ *This recipe makes a handful of fragrant bath beads. When one or two beads dissolve in warm bath water, they release skin-softening milk and oil, and the scent of roses.*

Makes 10 beads

> ¼ cup powdered milk
> 2 tablespoons white flour
> 2 tablespoons borax powder
> ¼ cup rose water
> 2 teaspoons mineral oil
> 10 drops rose fragrance oil
> 1 drop red food coloring (optional)

Combine the dried milk, flour, and borax in a bowl, stirring until well mixed. Add the rose water, mineral oil, rose fragrance oil, and food coloring (if desired). Stir until you have a thick dough. Take one teaspoon of dough and roll it into a ball, with your hands. Repeat until all of the dough has been shaped. Place the balls on a sheet of tin foil or waxed paper and let dry for twenty-four hours.

⬧ *To wrap the beads, place one in the center of a piece of four-inch by four-inch tissue paper or lace. Gather the edges together around the bead and tie with a piece of satin or curling ribbon.*

PEACHES AND CREAM BATH BEADS

The next time you take a warm, relaxing bath, try dropping one of these fragrant bath beads in the water. As the bead dissolves in your bath, the skin-softening milk and specially blended oils will be released, leaving your skin feeling silky smooth.

Makes 12 beads

> ¼ cup Epsom salts
> ⅓ cup white flour
> ¼ cup powdered milk
> 2 tablespoons distilled water
> 2 teaspoons sweet almond oil
> 2 teaspoons apricot kernel oil
> 10 drops peach fragrance oil
> 1 drop orange food coloring (optional)

Grind the Epsom salts into a fine powder in a food processor or crush with a mortar and pestle and place in a bowl. Add the flour and powdered milk to the salts and stir until well mixed. Add the water, almond oil, apricot kernel oil, fragrance oil, and food coloring (if desired) and stir until the mixture becomes doughlike. Knead the dough until the food coloring is evenly distributed. Roll teaspoonfuls of dough into balls, using the palms of your hands, and set on waxed paper. Let the beads dry for twenty-four hours.

❖ *Store Peaches and Cream Bath Beads in a cool, dry place, or wrap as suggested in the Rose Bath Beads recipe given earlier in this chapter.*
❖ *To make decorative designs on your beads, remove the paper from the end of a spool of thread and gently stamp the soft beads before they dry.*

PEPPERMINT BATH SALTS

....

◈ *For a relaxing bath, try adding a tablespoon of refreshing Peppermint Bath Salts to your warm bath water. Soothing peppermint has been used for hundreds of years to relieve headaches and sore muscles.*

Makes 4 ounces

> ½ cup Epsom salts
> ¼ teaspoon peppermint oil
> 1 drop red food coloring (optional)

Grind the Epsom salts to a fine powder in a food processor or crush with a mortar and pestle and pour into a bowl. Add the peppermint oil and food coloring (if desired) and stir until well mixed. Let the salts dry out overnight. Store in a tightly sealed jar.

◈ *To make Lemon Bath Salts, replace the peppermint oil with lemon oil and substitute yellow food coloring for the red.*

◈ *The pumice stone is one of nature's best scrubbers and is the perfect tool with which to remove rough and callused skin from the feet. Pumice is a soft stone that comes from volcanic lava. You can make your own oil-infused pumice stone that will release skin-softening oils while whisking away dry skin.*

> 1 natural pumice stone
>   (available at most health food stores)
> 2 tablespoons jojoba oil
> 10 drops vanilla fragrance oil
> 6 drops cinnamon oil

Place the pumice stone on a plate or in a bowl. In a small saucepan over low heat, warm the jojoba, vanilla, and cinnamon oils while stirring. Remove from the heat and stir the oils until well blended. Dip a cotton swab into the oil mixture and dab on the pumice stone. Continue until the stone is saturated and you have no more oil. Let the stone air dry for twenty-four hours before using. Your dried stone will have a fragrant smell and will release essential oils when used.

◈ *If your stone outlasts its fragrance, reapply oils as needed. For best results, use the stone on damp skin while soaking in the tub. Gently scrub rough spots with the stone.*

VANILLA DUSTING POWDER

For a cool, fresh feeling that will last all day, lightly dust yourself with this luxurious bath powder.

Makes 4 ounces

> ½ cup cornstarch
> 15 drops vanilla fragrance oil

Combine the cornstarch and fragrance oil in a large bowl and stir until the oil is evenly distributed and there are no lumps. Store in a cool place.

An old dusting powder box or a wooden cheese box make great powder containers. For a miniature shaker (ideal for gift giving), spoon the powder into a glass salt shaker and close the holes by placing a small piece of clear tape over them.

This naturally fragrant bath powder helps soak up excess moisture and keeps the skin feeling shower-fresh all day long.

Makes 5 ½ ounces

> ½ teaspoon dried mint leaves
> ½ cup cornstarch
> 2 tablespoons powdered green French clay
>   (or substitute powdered kaolin clay)
> 5 drops lemon oil
> 3 drops peppermint oil
> 3 drops grapefruit oil

Crush the mint leaves to a fine powder in a spice grinder; transfer the powder to a large bowl. Add the cornstarch and French clay and stir until well mixed. Add the oils and stir until evenly distributed. Store the powder in a cool place.

An old dusting powder box or a wooden cheese box make great powder containers. For a miniature shaker (ideal for gift giving), spoon the powder into a glass salt shaker and close the holes by placing a small piece of clear tape over them.

CHAPTER FOUR

For the Face

THE FACE mirrors the beauty we carry inside. The face is usually the first thing that others notice and the part of us they remember most. Special care of the face is important because it is constantly exposed to the elements and tends to take more abuse than the rest of the body. Beautiful complexions are sought after and can be enhanced by using the right products.

In the pages that follow, you'll find my original recipes for formulas specifically created for the care of the face. From hydrating moisturizers to tingling toners, these recipes are economical and make great gifts. After making and trying them, you may not go back to your regular products.

Floral Facial Cleanser is gentle and effective in removing dirt and make-up and leaves the face soft and smooth. Rub a small amount into the skin and wipe off with cotton balls.

Makes 3 ounces

> ¼ cup apricot kernel oil
> 1 teaspoon beeswax, grated
> 1 tablespoon rose water
> ½ teaspoon borax powder
> 4 drops rose fragrance oil (or fragrance oil of choice)

Warm the apricot kernel oil in a heavy saucepan over low heat and add the beeswax, stirring until dissolved and simmer. In another pan, heat the rose water and add the borax powder, stirring until dissolved. Slowly add the rose water mixture to the oil and beeswax mixture, while stirring with a wire whisk, until a thick cream forms and the mixture has cooled to room temperature. Add the rose fragrance oil and stir until well blended. Pour into a wide-mouthed jar and seal.

....

Aqua Moisturizer is specially formulated to provide the skin with vital moisture. Made with an aloe vera base, this moisturizer is ideal for facial use.

Makes 4 ounces

> ¼ cup aloe vera gel
> 2 tablespoons Lemon Meringue Pie Lotion
> (or substitute Vanilla Body Lotion; recipes
> on pages 3 and 8)

Combine the aloe vera gel and lotion in a bowl and stir with a wire whisk until smooth. Bottle.

Drench your skin with moisturizing aloe vera. This formula was designed to rehydrate and tone the skin. For best results, store in a spray bottle and mist it onto your face and body.

Makes 5 ounces

> ¼ cup distilled water
> 2 tablespoons orange flower water
> 2 tablespoons rose water
> 2 tablespoons aloe vera gel

Combine all of the ingredients in a spray bottle and shake until well mixed.

This soothing toner is made with invigorating Australian tea tree oil, which soothes the skin and discourages blemishes. Apply to the face after cleansing.

Makes 4 ounces

¼ cup witch hazel
¼ cup vodka
¼ teaspoon tea tree oil

Pour all of the ingredients into a bottle and shake until well mixed.

TINGLING MINT TONER

Tingling Mint Toner refreshes the skin, leaving it feeling cool and tingly clean. Witch hazel combined with peppermint oil and sugar (in the liqueur) helps tighten pores and shed dull skin cells. Dab on with cotton balls and leave on for ten minutes. Rinse with water.

Makes 4 ounces

¼ cup Peppermint Schnapps liqueur
¼ cup witch hazel
2 drops peppermint oil

Combine all ingredients in a bottle and shake until well mixed. Shake before use.

PEACH AND ROSE WATER FACIAL TONER

This formula is a gentle facial toner especially good for dry and sensitive skin. It tones and tightens without stinging or irritating the skin.

Makes 4 ounces

> ¼ cup rose water
> 2 tablespoons witch hazel
> 2 tablespoons vodka
> 5 drops peach fragrance oil

Combine all of the ingredients in a bottle and shake until well mixed. Apply with cotton balls or spritz onto the face with a spray bottle.

MINT MUD MASK

. . . .

Try a Mint Mud Mask facial for deep cleansing. As the mask dries it draws dirt and impurities from the skin. Peppermint helps to stabilize the skin and leaves it tingly clean.

Makes 5 ounces

> ¼ cup distilled water
> ¼ cup fuller's earth (or substitute with French clay)
> 2 tablespoons liquid glycerin
> 10 drops peppermint oil

In a saucepan, warm the water over low heat and add the fuller's earth, liquid glycerin, and peppermint oil. Stir until the mixture becomes a thick, smooth paste. Store in a wide-mouthed jar.

To use, apply a mask of the paste spreading a layer with your fingertips to the face (avoiding the eye area) and let dry. Rinse the mask off with warm water and pat dry.

If you plan to store this for a while, or give as a gift, add the peppermint oil directly to the fuller's earth and stir well. Let air dry overnight. Delete the glycerin from the recipe and give the powder with instructions to add an equal part water to powder before using.

. . . .

Things for Men

THIS CHAPTER is full of recipes that cater to the special needs of men. You'll find recipes for shaving cream, toner, deodorant, and other useful men's products. These specially designed formulas are perfect for gift giving. Try packaging one of each formula for a complete line of homemade skin and body care products for that lucky man. Or add a bottle of lotion or some of the other luxurious formulas from the previous chapters to complete your gift.

PEPPERMINT LATHERLESS SHAVING CREAM

....

This formula is specially designed for men. Made with real peppermint and skin-soothing aloe vera gel, this shaving cream soothes even the most sensitive skin and leaves it feeling soft and smooth.

Makes 4 ounces

⅓ cup aloe vera gel
2 tablespoons Peppermint Cream
(see recipe on page 10)

Combine the aloe vera gel and Peppermint Cream in a bowl and stir with a wire whisk until smooth. Store in a plastic squeeze bottle or a wide-mouthed jar.

Give as a gift with a razor and a bottle of Men's Aftershave Gel (see the next recipe).

....

. . . .

This special blend, made just for men, soothes and tones the skin after shaving. Made with pure aloe vera gel and nature's astringent witch hazel, this formula heals and soothes the skin. The essences of natural sandalwood and orange oil in this gel have a clean, woodsy fragrance.

Makes 6 ounces

½ cup aloe vera gel
2 tablespoons vodka
1 tablespoon orange flower water
2 teaspoons witch hazel
10 drops sandalwood oil
5 drops orange oil

Combine all of the ingredients in a bowl and stir with a wire whisk until well blended. Bottle.

. . . .

SANDALWOOD COLOGNE

The essence of natural sandalwood has been captured in this light cologne for men.

Makes 5 ounces

½ cup vodka
1 tablespoon jojoba oil
1 tablespoon rose water
10 drops sandalwood oil

Combine all of the ingredients in a bottle and shake until well mixed.

LAVENDER AND TEA TREE OIL FOOT POWDER

....

This recipe makes a powerful foot powder that is effective in handling foot odor and athlete's foot. Sprinkle on the feet daily.

Makes 2 ounces

¼ cup cornstarch
⅛ teaspoon tea tree oil
5 drops lavender oil

Combine all of the ingredients in a bowl and stir until well mixed and no lumps remain. Place the powder on a sheet of waxed paper and let air dry for twenty-four hours. When dry, remix the powder and store in a sealed container.

CHAPTER SIX

Colognes & Fragrances

MAKING YOUR own colognes and perfumes is simple and easy with my original recipes. Many perfumes on the market today are overpoweringly strong and can be quite expensive. By creating your own custom fragrances, you'll save money and enjoy chemical-free blends. All of my recipes are safe, gentle, and make excellent personalized gifts. After experimenting with a few of the recipes, you'll find it easy to dream up and produce your own delightful fragrances.

Bottled in fancy perfume atomizers and beautiful bottles, your homemade colognes will become treasured gifts.

Eau de Citrus is a fragrant, refreshing tonic. Spray it on and wear as a light cologne.

Makes 10 ounces

> ½ cup vodka
> ¼ cup distilled water
> 1 tablespoon orange flower water
> 10 drops lemon oil
> 2 drops orange oil

Combine the vodka, distilled water, and orange flower water in a saucepan and bring to a boil. Remove from heat and add the lemon oil and orange oil. Stir until well mixed. Let cool to room temperature and bottle.

AFTER BATH SPLASH

. . . .

This formula can be used after a bath or any time you want a light, refreshing fragrance. Add your favorite fragrance oil for a custom-scented splash.

Makes 10 ounces

½ cup distilled water
¼ cup vodka
15 drops fragrance oil
4 drops sandalwood oil

Combine all of the ingredients in a bottle and shake until well mixed. Store in a spray bottle or perfume atomizer.

PERFUME OILS

....

❖ *Making your own perfume oils is easy and economical. Since perfume oils need to be diluted before applying to the skin, follow the simple instructions given here.*

Makes ½ ounce

    1 tablespoon castor oil
    3 drops fragrance oil or essential oil
        (oils can also be mixed for a custom scent,
        for example, 1 drop peach, 1 drop raspberry,
        and 1 drop apple)

In a small container, add the drops of perfume oil to the castor oil and stir with a wooden toothpick. Store in small glass vials or miniature perfume bottles.

VICTORIAN VANILLA PERFUME

....

❖ *This light, sweetly scented perfume is perfect when you desire nothing more than a wisp of delicious fragrance. Victorian Vanilla Perfume makes the perfect gift for any woman, no matter what her tastes in perfume are.*

Makes 4½ ounces

> ¼ cup distilled water
> ¼ cup vodka
> 1 tablespoon pure vanilla extract
> 20 drops vanilla fragrance oil
> 3 drops sandalwood oil

Combine all of the ingredients and stir until well blended. Bottle in a perfume atomizer or spray bottle.

For a light, long-lasting cologne, follow these simple instructions. Make your own custom fragrances by adding your choice of perfume or essential oil.

Makes 4 ounces

¼ cup vodka
¼ cup distilled water
1 teaspoon jojoba oil
10 drops perfume or essential oil

Combine all of the ingredients in a bottle and shake until well mixed. Store in a spray bottle or perfume atomizer.

MOCK ROSE OR MOCK ORANGE FLOWER WATER

Real rose water and orange flower water are made by distilling fresh rose petals or orange blossoms in water. This recipe makes a similar product that's easy to prepare and costs just pennies a bottle.

Makes 2 ounces

> 2 tablespoons vodka
> 2 tablespoons distilled water
> 2 drops rose fragrance oil *or* orange oil

For Mock Rose Water, combine the vodka, distilled water, and rose fragrance oil in a small bottle and shake well to mix. For Mock Orange Flower Water, use orange oil in place of the rose fragrance oil.

Mock Rose Water and Mock Orange Flower Water are for use only in perfumery. Don't use them in cooking or as a substitute for real rose water or orange flower water in the recipes that call for them.

CHAPTER SEVEN

Other Luxuries

IN THIS chapter you'll find many recipes for useful and luxurious formulas. Did you know that you can make your own all-natural hair spray or soothing lip balm? Follow my easy recipes and create your own line of homemade toiletries.

There's nothing that bugs hate more than this all-natural insect repellent spray that's gentle enough to apply on the skin. Made with nature's bug repellent, citronella oil, this formula repels mosquitoes and fleas. Apply this pleasant-smelling spray on the skin before going outdoors. Reapply every six hours or after swimming.

Makes 5 ounces

> ½ cup vodka
> 2 tablespoons orange flower water
> 15 drops citronella oil
> 1 teaspoon jojoba oil

Combine all of the ingredients in a spray-pump bottle and shake until well mixed.

This nonstaining spray can also be used on furniture and carpet to repel fleas.

. . . .

◈ *Finally! An economical hair spray that's user friendly and friendly to the environ-ment. All-Natural Hair Spray contains no alcohol or harmful chemicals.*

Makes 6 ounces

> ½ cup distilled water
> 2 tablespoons light corn syrup
> 10 drops fragrance oil (optional)

Bring the water to a boil and stir in the corn syrup until dissolved. Remove from heat and stir in the fragrance oil (if desired). Let cool to room temperature and store in a spray-pump bottle.

REFRESHING FOOT SPRAY

. . . .

This remedy soothes tired, achy feet. Tea tree oil and sandalwood in an alcohol base help to combat foot odor. Store in a spray-pump bottle and mist onto feet any time they need a refreshing lift.

Makes 6 ounces

> ½ cup vodka
> ¼ cup witch hazel
> ½ teaspoon tea tree oil
> 10 drops sandalwood oil

Combine all of the ingredients in a spray-pump bottle and shake until well mixed. Shake before use for even oil distribution.

Refreshing Foot Spray can be sprayed through stockings.

LAVENDER DEODORANT SPRAY

This recipe makes a pleasant-smelling spray that helps combat underarm odor. Lavender Deodorant Spray is powerful enough for men, too.

Makes 3 ounces

> ¼ cup vodka
> 2 tablespoons witch hazel
> 10 drops lavender oil
> 2 drops lemon oil

Combine all of the ingredients in a spray-pump bottle and shake until well mixed. Shake before use.

MINTY MOUTHWASH

This alcohol-free mouthwash is a treat to the taste buds and helps fight germs and bacteria that can cause bad breath.

Makes 10 ounces

> 1 cup distilled water
> 2 teaspoons liquid glycerin
> 1 teaspoon witch hazel
> 1 teaspoon aloe vera gel
> 7 drops peppermint oil
> 5 drops cinnamon oil

In a saucepan, bring the water to a boil and stir in the liquid glycerin, witch hazel, and aloe vera gel. Remove the pan from the heat and add the peppermint and cinnamon oils. Let cool to room temperature and bottle.

GELATIN NAIL SOAK

....

This old-fashioned remedy will help to strengthen and harden brittle or weak fingernails if used regularly. Soak your nails once a week for best results.

Makes 5 ounces (enough for one treatment)

> ½ cup distilled water
> 1 tablespoon unflavored gelatin

In a saucepan, bring the distilled water to a boil and add the gelatin, stirring until dissolved. Remove from heat. Place the mixture in a bowl and let cool to room temperature. Immerse your fingertips in the mixture and let soak for 20 minutes. Afterward, wash your hands with soap and water and discard the left-over treatment.

Remove nail polish before using this remedy.

SUPER NAIL TREATMENT

....

Your fingernails will soak up this Super Nail Treatment; it is specially designed to strengthen nails and discourage infection.

Makes ½ ounce

>   1 tablespoon jojoba oil
>   ¼ teaspoon tea tree oil
>   5 drops lemon oil

In a small bowl, combine all three ingredients and stir until well mixed. Pour the mixture into an empty nail polish bottle, close, and label. Brush Super Nail Treatment on your nails twice a week before going to bed.

LEMON LIP BALM

Lemon Lip Balm protects and softens the lips.

Makes ½ ounce

> 1 tablespoon petroleum jelly
> ½ teaspoon beeswax, grated
> 3 drops lemon oil

In a very small pot, heat the petroleum jelly and add the beeswax, stirring until melted. Remove from the heat and stir in the lemon oil. Pour the mixture into a small screw-top jar or metal tin.

PEPPERMINT LIP GLOSS

Mint Lip Gloss protects and softens your lips. For incredible shine, apply this lip gloss with a small brush.

Makes 1 ounce

> 1 tablespoon castor oil
> 1 tablespoon liquid glycerin
> 1 teaspoon liquid lanolin
> 5 drops peppermint oil (optional)

Combine all four ingredients in a small bowl and stir until well blended. Store in a small screw-top jar.

CHAPTER EIGHT

Gift Wrapping

Presenting and Displaying Your Gifts

CREATIVE PACKAGING of your homemade toiletries makes your gift even more special. By wrapping your creations decoratively, you can make your already spectacular gifts look even more appealing and fabulous. The ideas in this section will help you to present your gifts safely and beautifully.

Bottles

Bottles are perfect for storing lotions, creams, perfumes, and other liquid luxuries. You can find bottles in many different shapes and sizes, from plain plastic to fancy perfume atomizers. I've found beautiful glass bottles in shades of blue and even fuchsia. I fill the bottles with my liquid creations and tie a beautiful ribbon around the bottle neck. Gold French ribbon and brightly colored satin ribbons look really spectacular. To create a natural look you can tie a piece of raffia around the top. For an elegant touch, hang a fancy tassle on your bottle. Antique-style perfume atomizers make wonderful containers for perfumes. You can order bottles and atomizers by mail or buy them from import shops. Silk flowers add a nice touch to your bottled creations. You can slip their stems under your piece of ribbon that will hold them securely in place.

Old bottles can be recycled and reused. To remove paper labels, fill a large bowl with warm water and about an ounce of dish-washing liquid. Drop in the bottle and let it soak for a few hours. The old labels should lift off. Scrub off any glue residue with a vegetable brush. To remove silk-screened printing from a bottle, dab on an acetone nail polish remover with some cotton balls. Last year I made an assortment of homemade perfumes and lotions as a gift for a friend. I filled miniature perfume bottles with my own custom blends and filled several travel-size shampoo bottles with lotions and creams. Each bottle was labeled and had a thin piece of colorful satin ribbon tied around the top. For another friend I made a "country" theme assortment of lotions and bath oils and put them in small jelly jars. Each jar top was covered with a circle of gingham fabric and tied with a matching ribbon. I wrote my labels by hand to give each jar a casual, cozy look.

Labeling

You should always label your products, whether giving them as gifts or keeping them for yourself. Write the name of the product (for example, "Lemon Meringue Pie Lotion") on the label and secure it to the container. You can use plain white labels or purchase decorative labels. To waterproof your labels, rub a white candle firmly over the writing. This leaves a wax coating that will help prevent ink smears if it gets wet.

You can also make beautiful decoupage labels using plain, white computer labels. Cut out pictures from magazines of flowers and other images that you like. Using spray glue, spray the back side of the cut-outs and press them around the edges of the label, leaving enough space in the center of the label on which to write. You can also use stickers such as metallic stars or zany designs.

Paints and paint pens can be used to write directly on the bottles. Make sure that the paint you choose will stick to the type of bottle you've chosen. Another good idea is to list the ingredients used in the product on the labeling. This will help friends avoid using a product to which they're allergic. Finally, write any special usage instructions on your label; for example, if a specific amount is suggested, you might write "add 1 tablespoon to warm bath water."

Fancy Boxes

Packaging your creations in fancy boxes doesn't have to cost a fortune. You can turn an ordinary shoe box into a treasured gift by covering it with self-sticking fabric or by using simple decoupage techniques. I sometimes cover shoe boxes with decorative contact paper and have even used wall paper with interesting patterns. Boxes can also be spray painted. Metallic gold and silver are perfect colors to use around the holidays. For more ideas, get a book about box decorating, which you can find at craft and fabric stores.

Sealing and Packing

Proper sealing and packing are vital if you plan to mail your creations. Always make sure that caps and lids are securely closed. To seal a cork-type bottle, the cork should fit snugly. Use a glue gun around the edges (the glue will peel off when the cork is removed).

When packing gift baskets or boxes, choose a basket or box that your creations fit into with very little room to shift around. Cushion any empty spaces with wadded-up tissue paper, bubble wrap, or raffia packing material. Then seal the box. The contents should not move around inside if you've packed them well. Give the box a test shake before mailing. Always mark your boxes "fragile" or "this end up" to ensure that they arrive safely.

Other Ideas

Luxury gift sets make impressive gifts and are inexpensive. Fill a box with an assortment of bath products and add a tea cup with some tea bags.

Theme baskets are another type of gift to make. Fill a basket with lotions and bath products all of the same scent, such as rose or lemon. Tuck a few silk flowers in with your package. To hold your bottles in place, use raffia packing material. It comes in many bright colors and will look great! Once you've packed your basket, use a large piece of cellophane to wrap the entire basket and secure it with a large, colorful ribbon. Cellophane gift wrap can be found with regular wrapping paper in the stores and comes in many bright colors as well as clear.

A great way to wrap dry or powdered luxuries such as bath powder and bath salts is to make your own envelopes. Take a regular envelope and unfold it to use as a pattern. Lay it on a piece of decorative wrapping paper and trace the edges. Cut the wrapping paper and fold it into an envelope, using tape to secure the edges and seams. Fill it with powder or bath salt and seal. Stick a pretty label on the outside of the envelope.

Marketplace

SOME OF the ingredients and supplies for making cosmetics at home can be hard to find if you don't live in a big city. The following are listings of manufacturers and suppliers who sell cosmetic supplies by mail.

Aroma Vera
5901 Rodeo Rd.
Los Angeles, California 90016-4312
Essential oils, aromatherapy supplies, floral waters

General Bottle Supply
P.O. Box 58734
Vernon, California 90058-0734
Bottles, lids, droppers

General Wax and Candle Company
P.O. Box 9398
North Hollywood, California 91609
Beeswax, molds, candle-making supplies

Grandma's Spice Shop
P.O. Box 472
Odenton, Maryland 21113
Oils, herbs, clays

Hagenow Laboratories
1302 Washington St.
Manitowoc, Wisconsin 54220
Waxes, oils, pH kits

Lorann Oils
4518 Aurelius Rd.
P.O. Box 22009
Lansing, Michigan 48909-2009
Perfume oils, soap-, candy- and candle-making supplies

Meadowood Cottage
P.O. Box 86042
Portland, Oregon 97286
Essential and perfume oils

Mountain Rose Herbs
P.O. Box 2000
Redway, California 95560
*Herbs, oils, bottles, clays, labels, books, aloe vera,
lanolin, glycerin, beeswax, floral waters*

Pourette
P.O. Box 15220
6910 Roosevelt Way N.E.
Seattle, Washington 98115
Soap- and candle-making supplies, unscented soap

Sunfeather Herbal Soap Company, Inc.
1551 State Highway 72
Potsdam, New York 13676
Soap-making supplies, essential oils

Valley Hills Press
1864 Ridgeland Rd.
Starkville, Massachusetts 39759
Books about soap making

Victorian Essence
P.O. Box 3497
Glendale, California 91221-0497
Shampoo concentrate and shampoo-making kits

INDEX

Jams, Jellies & Preserves

Linda Ferrari

Linda Ferrari shares the secrets of canning the perfect jams, jellies, and preserves as well as innovative ideas for wrapping and packaging so that anyone you present them to will feel charmed, flattered, and loved! Includes recipes for Frangelico Fig Jam, Pomegranate–Kiwi Jelly, Currant and Quince Jam, and Old-Fashioned Blackberry Preserves.

Salsas, Chutneys & Relishes

Linda Ferrari

*R*evealing the secrets of classic salsas, chutneys, and relishes, Linda Ferrari presents everyone's favorite recipes and a host of thoroughly modern recipes too. Ferrari also presents ways to personalize and decorate your homemade gifts with the distinct love and warmth of a bygone era. Includes recipes for Apple–Walnut Chutney, Festive Cranberry Relish, and Jicama and Chili Salsa.

Soaps, Shampoos & Other Suds

Kelly Reno

*I*magine the most simple ingredients—herbs, flowers, and pure soaps.
Kelly Reno shows you how to work magic with these natural basics and turn
them into indulgent treasures. These are simple, yet divine recipes made from
the freshest ingredients. Includes recipes for Coffee and Cream Soap,
Georgia Peach Shower Gel, and Peppermint Clarifying Shampoo.

FILL IN AND MAIL TODAY

PRIMA PUBLISHING
P.O. Box 1260BK
Rocklin, CA 95677

USE YOUR VISA/MC AND ORDER BY PHONE **(916) 632-4400**
Monday–Friday 9 A.M.–4 P.M. PST

I'd like to order copies of the following titles:

Quantity	Title	Amount
_____	*Jams, Jellies & Preserves* $12	_____
_____	*Salsas, Chutneys & Relishes* $12	_____
_____	*Oils, Lotions & Other Luxuries* $12	_____
_____	*Soaps, Shampoos & Other Suds* $12	_____
	Subtotal	_____
	Postage & Handling ($5 for first book, $.50 for additional books)	_____
	7.25% Sales Tax (CA)	_____
	5% Sales Tax (IN and MD)	_____
	8.25% Sales Tax (TN)	_____
	TOTAL (U.S. funds only)	_____

Hawaii, Canada, Foreign, and Priority Request orders, please call 632-4400

Check enclosed for $_____ (payable to Prima Publishing)
Charge my   ❑ MasterCard   ❑ Visa
Account No. _____   Exp. Date _____
Signature _____
Your Name _____
Address _____
City/State/Zip _____ Daytime Telephone (___) _____